I0774644

THERAPEUTIC GALLOP

Discover the Power of Equine Therapy

Aura Hípica

CONTENTS

INTRODUCTION TO EQUINE THERAPY

Equine therapy, also known as equestrian intervention, is a multidisciplinary and transformative field that combines the art of horsemanship, equine care and specialized therapeutic methods to enhance the physical, emotional, cognitive and social well-being of individuals. This unique approach is based on the dynamic interaction between human and horse, establishing an exceptional bond that acts as a bridge to healing and personal growth.

Beyond riding, this therapeutic approach includes a wide range of activities ranging from direct contact with horses to performing specific tasks such as brushing, feeding and handling. Each of these interactions is designed to address specific needs and foster holistic development in those who participate.

The relationship with horses brings obvious physical benefits, such as improved balance, coordination and muscle strength, but also opens doors to self-discovery, overcoming emotional challenges and fostering social skills. This therapeutic model combines the warmth, empathy and sensitivity of equines to create a safe and nurturing environment in which people can explore and reach their full potential.

Throughout this book, we will explore the fundamentals, benefits and applications of this method, highlighting how the connection with horses has become a key tool for holistic wellness and human development. This journey seeks not only to inform, but also to inspire understanding and appreciation of the extraordinary role these animals play in our lives and on the road to recovery.

ITS ORIGINS

The use of horses as allies in human healing and wellness has millennia-old roots. Since ancient times, these animals have been valued not only for their strength and capacity for work, but also for the positive impact they had on people. In the Greek civilization, Hippocrates, known as the father of medicine, mentioned in his writings the benefits of horseback riding to improve physical and emotional health, highlighting how this activity strengthened the body and promoted mental balance.

During the Middle Ages, horses continued to be symbols of power and nobility, and although there was no formal therapeutic approach, interactions with these animals were part of everyday life. At this time, it was recognized that the relationship with horses could influence character and emotional development, especially in young men of the aristocratic classes who learned horseback riding as part of their training.

The renaissance of horseback riding as a therapeutic activity began to take shape in the 18th century, with the first attempts to document its impact on health. In England, some physicians and philosophers began to observe the benefits that horses offered in terms of mobility and emotional well-being for people with physical disabilities. However, it was in the 20th century that equine therapy began to gain formal recognition.

Advances in the 20th century

The real push came after the World Wars, when horses played a crucial role in the recovery of wounded soldiers. In rehabilitation hospitals, it was observed how riding and caring for horses helped veterans regain mobility, confidence and emotional balance. This experience inspired researchers and health professionals to further study the therapeutic potential of these interactions.

One of the key milestones was the work of Lis Hartel, a Danish rider who, after becoming partially paralyzed due to polio, used horseback riding as part of her recovery process. Her success in winning a silver medal at the 1952 Olympics in horsemanship sparked global interest in equine therapy applications. This landmark case marked the beginning of a new era for the practice.

Formalization and expansion

During the 1960s and 1970s, the development of international organizations dedicated to equine-assisted therapies, such as the Federation for Therapeutic Riding International (FRDI), helped to standardize methodologies and establish criteria for the training of therapists and horses. Countries such as England, France and Canada were pioneers in implementing specialized programs that integrated this modality in rehabilitation and special education centers.

In France, equestrian reeducation took a medical approach starting in 1965, establishing an interdisciplinary model that included physiotherapists, psychologists and animal behaviorists. In England, the founding of the first therapeutic riding association in 1956 consolidated a formal framework for the practice. Meanwhile, in Canada and the United States, centers dedicated exclusively to equine-assisted therapy began to emerge, focusing on the care of people with physical and cognitive disabilities.

At the present time

Today, this therapeutic approach has evolved into a global practice backed by scientific research that supports its benefits. The combination of traditional knowledge with modern advances in physiotherapy, psychology and neuroscience has allowed the development of increasingly personalized and effective programs. Its success lies in the horses' ability to generate a unique emotional connection, acting as mirrors of human emotions and catalysts for physical and psychological recovery.

This historical journey not only highlights the impact of horses on healing over the centuries, but also reaffirms their place as indispensable allies on the path to holistic wellness. Their presence continues to be a source of inspiration, transformation and hope for millions of people around the world.

MULTIDIMENSIONAL BENEFITS

The equine therapeutic approach offers a variety of benefits that span multiple areas of human well-being, making it a transformative tool. Among the physical benefits is the ability of the horse's three-dimensional movement to simulate human gait. This feature helps improve the rider's balance and coordination, strengthens the musculature, especially in the trunk and limbs, and increases flexibility and range of motion. In addition, the horse's body heat acts as a natural compress, relaxing muscles and relieving tension, which is especially useful in cases of spasticity or tension associated with neurological disorders.

In terms of **emotional benefits**, interaction with horses generates a safe environment that reduces anxiety and stress. Overcoming the challenges posed during the sessions fosters self-esteem and self-confidence, while the emotional bond with these animals facilitates the regulation of emotions, helping participants to recognize and manage their feelings more effectively.

On the other hand, **cognitive benefits** include the development of concentration and sustained attention, fundamental for both learning and daily life. Activities structured around the handling and care of the horse stimulate planning and problem-solving skills, while reinforcing memory and the ability to organize tasks effectively.

Socially, this practice also has a significant impact. Participants improve their **verbal and nonverbal communication**, develop empathy and respect for others, and learn to cooperate in group activities, which is especially valuable for those who face challenges in their social interactions.

Because of this multidimensional nature, equine-assisted therapy is applied in a wide variety of contexts, including developmental disorders such as autism spectrum disorder, neurological conditions such as cerebral palsy, emotional difficulties such as anxiety or post-traumatic stress disorder, and learning difficulties such as dyslexia. Each session is carefully designed to meet the specific needs of the participant, tailored to their abilities and goals.

Beyond its therapeutic effects, the connection with horses offers an experience of self-discovery and personal transformation. This approach not only addresses specific symptoms, but inspires holistic change, allowing people to explore their potential and strengthen their bond with the natural environment.

THE RELATIONSHIP WITH THE HORSE: A THERAPEUTIC LINK

The core of equine-assisted therapy lies in the unique and deeply meaningful relationship that develops between the participant and the animal. This connection transcends everyday interactions, becoming a therapeutic bond that acts as a catalyst for personal and emotional change. Horses, with their innate sensitivity and ability to pick up on even the most subtle signals of human emotional states, provide **immediate feedback** that honestly reflects the participant's emotions and behaviors.

The horse as an emotional mirror

One of the most salient features of this relationship is that the horse acts as a **living emotional mirror**. Equines not only perceive human emotions, but respond to them authentically and without judgment. For example, a horse may become restless in the face of its rider's anxiety or calm in the face of a serene attitude. This direct and immediate response allows participants to identify and recognize their own emotions, often in ways they had not previously considered.

This interaction fosters a **profound process of self-knowledge**. By observing how the horse reacts to his emotional state, the participant acquires a new perspective on his behavior and feelings. This awareness becomes a valuable tool for working on aspects such as stress management, emotional regulation and overcoming internal barriers.

A safe and non-judgmental environment

The non-judgmental nature of the horse is one of the fundamental pillars of its therapeutic effectiveness. In their interaction with these animals, participants find a safe space where they can express themselves freely without fear of criticism or rejection. This trusting environment is especially beneficial for people dealing with emotional problems, such as anxiety, post-traumatic stress disorder or depression.

The simple act of caring for, petting or guiding a horse can become a deeply healing experience. These actions foster a sense of accomplishment and connection that builds **self-esteem** and **self-confidence**, while the ongoing relationship with the horse teaches lessons in patience, empathy and responsibility.

Non-verbal communication and emotional learning

The relationship with the horse is largely based on **non-verbal communication**, which allows the development of perception skills and emotional connection. Gestures such as touching, leading or riding generate a shared language between the participant and the animal, reinforcing the bond and promoting meaningful emotional learning. This communication process helps participants become more aware of their own emotions and how they impact their environment.

The horse as an active therapeutic agent

The horse is not simply a therapeutic medium, but an **active agent in the healing process**. Its ability to provide authentic and constant feedback challenges the participant to reflect and adjust, promoting tangible personal growth. Every interaction with the horse, from learning to interpret its behavior to effectively guiding it, reinforces essential skills such as resilience, self-regulation and self-confidence.

Impact beyond the sessions

The impact of this relationship is not limited to therapeutic sessions. Participants often transfer what they learn to their daily lives, applying the lessons of self-confidence, emotional control and empathy in their personal and professional relationships. This transformation makes the horse a true guide to holistic wellness, helping individuals overcome challenges and achieve greater balance in their lives.

In conclusion, the relationship between horse and participant is much more than an interaction; it is a bridge to healing, growth and personal transformation. This bond, based on trust, sensitivity and empathy, stands out as one of the most powerful and unique aspects of equine-assisted therapy.

Key Elements

Effective implementation of equine-assisted therapy requires a combination of carefully coordinated factors, each playing an essential role in the success of the therapeutic process. These elements not only ensure the safety and well-being of participants, but also maximize the benefits that this modality can offer.

One of the fundamental pillars is the proper selection of the horse. Not all equines are suitable for this type of work; it is crucial that the animal has a docile temperament, tolerance to variable environments and a calm disposition to unexpected stimuli, such as involuntary movements or loud sounds from the participants. In addition, they should be trained specifically for therapeutic activities, which includes being accustomed to constant physical contact and responding predictably to the therapist's cues.

The next essential component is the training and experience of the therapeutic team. This multidisciplinary group includes professionals in areas such as occupational therapy, physical therapy, psychology and equine management. Their specialized knowledge allows them to design and implement sessions that address both the physical and emotional aspects of the participants. In addition, it is essential that the team has experience in interpreting the horse's responses, as these animals provide key signals about the rider's emotional and physical state.

The environment in which the therapy takes place is also crucial. A safe and controlled environment ensures that both the participant and the horse can interact safely. This involves having adequate facilities, such as enclosed arenas and stable surfaces, as well as safety equipment, including helmets and harnesses when necessary. Constant supervision by the therapeutic team ensures that any unforeseen events can be handled immediately.

Another indispensable factor is the personalization of therapeutic plans. Each participant has unique needs and goals, so sessions must be individually designed. This includes choosing specific activities, such as riding, brushing or leading the horse, and tailoring them to the individual's physical, emotional or cognitive abilities. These adaptations allow the therapy to be effective, focusing on areas such as improving balance, emotional strengthening or developing social skills.

Together, these key elements work in harmony to ensure that equine-assisted therapy is not only safe and effective, but also a transformative experience. By combining proper horse selection, a well-prepared team, a safe environment and personalized plans, this therapeutic modality achieves its full potential, providing participants with a path to holistic healing and growth.

CONCLUSION

Equine therapy represents an extraordinary fusion between human and equine, where the transformative power of this relationship opens unique pathways to healing, personal growth and holistic wellness. This therapeutic approach not only addresses physical, emotional, cognitive and social needs, but also inspires a deep respect for the special bond we share with animals.

By focusing on the holistic well-being of participants, this modality not only improves their quality of life, but also redefines our understanding of the therapeutic potential of equines. Interacting with these noble companions allows us to explore new ways to connect with our emotions, overcome personal challenges and achieve meaningful goals. Each session becomes a unique experience, tailored to individual needs, but always anchored in trust, empathy and mutual respect.

Entering the world of equine-assisted therapy is to open a door to infinite possibilities, where the human-equine bond acts as a powerful tool for change. This journey not only benefits those directly involved, but also enriches our perspective on the ability of animals to influence our lives in a positive and lasting way. With this practice, not only is the body and mind transformed, but a renewed sense of purpose and connection to the natural environment is awakened. This is the beginning of a journey of self-discovery, growth and healing, guided by the sensitivity and strength of one of mankind's most exceptional companions: the horse.

FUNDAMENTALS OF EQUINE THERAPY

Equine-assisted therapy is based on a combination of disciplines that, when integrated, offer a unique and effective approach to human welfare. This multidisciplinary practice draws from areas such as **psychology, veterinary medicine, occupational therapy** and **physiotherapy**, among others, managing to address the needs of the individual from an integral and holistic perspective.

First, **psychology** provides an essential framework for understanding the emotions, behaviors and relational dynamics that arise in interaction with horses. Professionals in this area design therapeutic strategies that allow participants to explore and regulate their emotions, while working on goals related to self-esteem, confidence and stress management.

On the other hand, **veterinary medicine** ensures the health and well-being of the horse, a central element in the success of this therapy. The horses used in this approach must not only be physically healthy, but also emotionally balanced to respond appropriately and predictably to the needs of the participant. This comprehensive care includes constant check-ups, proper feeding and specific training that prepares the equine for its therapeutic role.

Occupational therapy adds to the process by focusing on the development of functional skills. Here, the activities designed with the horses seek strengthen independence, improve coordination and encourage motor planning in the participants. This is especially important for people with physical or neurological limitations, who find these sessions an effective and motivating way to advance towards their goals.

Finally, **physical therapy** plays a crucial role by taking advantage of the horse's three-dimensional movement, which mimics the human gait pattern. This unique physical stimulus helps strengthen muscles, improve balance and posture, as well as promote mobility in people with physical conditions.

Working together, these disciplines form a **cohesive and comprehensive system** that transforms the interaction with the horse into a holistic therapeutic resource. This chapter explores how each of these areas specifically contributes to the overall impact of equine-assisted therapy, demonstrating that its success lies in this synergy between expertise and approaches.

THE CENTRAL ROLE OF THE HORSE

Horses are much more than just facilitators in equine-assisted therapy; their role is fundamental, as they act as active partners and agents of change in the therapeutic process. Recognized for their strength, beauty and sensitivity, these animals possess a unique ability to establish deep and meaningful connections with humans, making them the heart of this therapeutic modality.

Equine Empathy

Horses' natural empathy is one of their most outstanding qualities in this context. Their innate ability to **perceive and respond to human emotions** allows them to act as emotional mirrors. This characteristic means that the horse reflects the participant's emotions authentically and without judgment. For example, if the rider is anxious or insecure, the horse may become restless, while a calm and confident attitude from the rider generates a calm response from the animal. This interaction encourages emotional awareness, as participants can recognize their own internal states and work on their emotional regulation.

Equine empathy not only allows participants to explore their feelings, but also creates a safe space where they can address fears, insecurities or emotional challenges. This authentic connection facilitates deep personal growth, helping participants develop self-regulation skills and overcome emotional barriers.

Non-Verbal Communication

Horses are masters of **nonverbal communication**, conveying their emotional states and reactions through movements, facial expressions and body postures. By interacting with these animals, participants learn to interpret these subtle signals, developing a greater awareness of their own body language and the impact it has on their relationships.

Interacting with horses promotes the development of **more empathetic communication skills**, as it requires a genuine connection based on observation, respect and reciprocity. This learning not only enhances the relationship with horses, but also translates into more effective and meaningful human relationships. By relying on body language and energy to communicate with the horse, participants acquire valuable tools to improve their interaction with others, strengthening their personal and social bonds.

An active and transformative facilitator

The horse is not simply a means to achieve the therapeutic objectives, but an **active agent in the process of change**. Its constant presence and response forces the participant to be present in the moment, to adjust his behavior and to reflect on his emotions and attitudes. This process transforms the relationship between horse and human into a mutual learning experience, where both contribute to growth and healing.

In conclusion, the horse is not only the center of this therapy because of its physical characteristics, but also because of its ability to connect deeply with people, reflect their emotions and act as a guide on the path to self-knowledge and transformation. Its central role is the very soul of equine-assisted therapy, as it offers an experience that is not only therapeutic, but also deeply human.

BASIC PRINCIPLES OF HUMAN-ANIMAL INTERACTION

The therapeutic interaction between humans and horses is based on a set of fundamental principles that ensure both the well-being of the equine and the effectiveness of the therapeutic process. These principles, centered on mutual respect, safety and effective communication, are essential to establish a genuine and transformative bond between the participant and the horse.

Mutual Respect

Respect is the basis of any therapeutic relationship with horses. This principle implies recognizing the horse as a living being with its own physical and emotional needs, and not simply as a therapeutic tool. The welfare of the horse must be a constant priority, ensuring that it is physically and emotionally prepared to participate in the sessions. This respect fosters **an environment of safety and comfort**, where the horse can interact naturally and freely with the participants, allowing the relationship to develop in an authentic and balanced way.

Security and Confidence

Safety is a fundamental pillar of any human-horse interaction. Creating a safe environment includes ensuring that facilities are adequate, horses are trained for therapeutic situations, and participants are properly supervised. This environment not only physically protects both parties, but also facilitates the development of **mutual trust**. Trust, once established, allows the participant to feel comfortable exploring their emotions and abilities, while the horse responds in a calm and predictable manner, creating an enriching therapeutic experience.

Clear Communication

The relationship between participant and horse depends heavily on **effective and consistent communication**. Unlike humans, horses communicate primarily through body language and energy, which requires participants to learn to be aware of their own movements, postures and attitudes. This form of non-verbal communication fosters an authentic connection, based on observation and mutual understanding.

The role of the therapist is key in this aspect, especially in the early stages of the interaction. Therapists act as mediators, helping the participant to interpret the horse's signals and convey clear instructions. This process not only facilitates the human-animal relationship, but also teaches the participant communication skills that can be applied in other aspects of his or her life.

Synergy in interaction

When these principles are consistently applied, a synergistic relationship is created between human and horse. Mutual respect establishes a foundation of equality and reciprocity, safety provides a framework of trust, and clear communication allows for a deep and meaningful connection. Together, these elements maximize the therapeutic benefits, making the interaction a transformative experience for both the participant and the equine.

ETHICS AND WELFARE

The welfare of horses is a fundamental pillar in equine-assisted therapy. These animals are not only active participants in the therapeutic process, but also living beings whose health and balance must be always preserved. To achieve this, professionals working in this field must adhere to strict ethical standards that guarantee the equine's integral care, from its physical health to its emotional and social well-being.

Integral Care

Proper care of horses encompasses complete care that includes both their physical and emotional needs. On the physical side, it is essential to provide them with a **balanced diet**, adapted to their age, activity and state of health, as well as constant access to clean water. **Regular exercise** is also indispensable, not only to maintain their physical condition, but also to release accumulated energy and prevent behavioral problems.

Emotionally and socially, horses need interaction with other equines to reinforce their gregarious nature, as they are herd animals by nature. Likewise, respectful and stress-free handling should be ensured in every activity, allowing the horse to participate in therapeutic sessions in a balanced state of mind. In addition, **regular veterinary check-ups** and preventive care are essential to ensure that the horse is in optimal condition to perform its therapeutic role.

Rest and Recovery

A crucial aspect of equine welfare is ensuring **adequate rest**. Horses participating in therapeutic programs must have sufficient time to recover between sessions, avoiding physical or mental exhaustion. This includes setting clear limits on the number of daily and weekly working hours, as well as scheduling full rest days to allow them to relax and recharge.

Rest not only protects the horse's long-term health, but also ensures the sustainability of the therapeutic program. An exhausted or stressed horse will not be able to perform its role effectively and could experience physical or emotional health problems that compromise its well-being. Therefore, practitioners must be careful to assess the individual capabilities of each horse, adjusting the workload according to its specific needs.

Ethical commitment in equine therapy

Adherence to these ethical principles is not only a professional obligation, but also a reflection of respect and gratitude towards these animals that contribute so much to human welfare. The relationship between humans and horses in the therapeutic context should be mutually beneficial, ensuring that the horse not only contributes to the therapeutic process, but also enjoys a healthy and balanced life.

Ultimately, ethics in equine therapy goes beyond compliance; it is about valuing the horse as a partner and collaborator, ensuring its well-being in all aspects. This approach not only protects the equine, but also strengthens the quality and effectiveness of the therapy, allowing this special bond between human and horse to be truly transformative.

CONCLUSION

The fundamentals of equine-assisted therapy highlight the richness and depth of this practice, showing how a well-structured human-equine relationship can bring about significant changes in people's lives. By integrating disciplines such as psychology, physical therapy, occupational therapy and veterinary medicine, this therapeutic modality takes a truly holistic approach, where body, mind and emotions are addressed together.

The **role of the horse** in this therapy is much more than instrumental; its sensitivity, empathy and capacity for emotional connection make it an active agent in the process of healing and personal growth. Likewise, the **principles of human-animal interaction**, based on mutual respect, trust and effective communication, are essential to establish a bond that is not only therapeutic, but also transformative for both parties.

On the other hand, **ethical and welfare standards** ensure that this practice is sustainable and respectful, not only protecting the horse, but also optimizing therapeutic outcomes for participants. By prioritizing the equine's physical and emotional health, the balance necessary for this therapy to be effective and humanely responsible is reinforced.

Ultimately, this holistic approach not only improves the quality of life for participants, but also enriches our understanding of the human-animal connection. Equine-assisted therapy has established itself as a unique and powerful modality, capable of transforming lives by harnessing the extraordinary bond that emerges between people and these noble companions. This practice represents not only a path to wellness, but also a reminder of the importance of empathy, respect and cross-species collaboration.

PREPARATION FOR EQUINE THERAPY

Preparation for equine-assisted therapy is an integral and essential process that guarantees both the effectiveness and safety of this therapeutic modality. This preliminary stage is key, as it establishes the foundations on which the program will be developed, allowing them to adequately address the individual needs of the participants, the conditions and welfare of the horses, as well as the preparation and coordination of the therapeutic team.

In this chapter, we will explore in detail the fundamental elements that are part of this preparation, approaching each aspect from a holistic perspective. The **preparatory phase** not only ensures that therapeutic goals are achievable, but also promotes an environment of respect and professionalism that benefits everyone involved.

The importance of this preparation lies in the balance between careful planning and flexibility to adapt to the unique needs of each session, achieving an enriching and safe experience for participants and equines. This approach establishes a solid foundation for successful therapy, allowing sessions to run smoothly, effectively and sustainably.

SELECTING THE RIGHT HORSE

The choice of horse is one of the fundamental elements in the preparation for equine-assisted therapy. Not all horses possess the necessary qualities to play this role, and their selection requires a careful analysis based on specific criteria that guarantee both their welfare and the effectiveness of the therapeutic sessions.

Temperament

A horse intended for therapy must have an **exceptionally calm and patient temperament**. These qualities are essential to handle the various unpredictable situations that may arise during sessions, such as involuntary movements or unexpected sounds from participants. The equine's friendly disposition and tolerance to interact with different people, including those with physical or emotional limitations, make it a reliable and effective therapeutic companion.

Horses with balanced temperaments act as an emotional support point for participants, providing a sense of security and stability. Their ability to adapt to the individual needs of each person in the sessions is crucial to therapeutic success.

Health and Physical Conditions

The health of the horse is an indispensable pillar. Only horses in **optimal physical condition** can safely participate in therapeutic programs. This includes strong musculature, a healthy bone structure and an adequate energy level to support the activities without risk of injury. Regular veterinary check-ups, as well as a balanced diet and proper exercise regimen, are essential components to keeping equines in top condition.

In addition, the horses selected must be carefully evaluated for any physical or emotional problems that may compromise their performance in the therapeutic environment. A healthy horse not only ensures their well-being, but also ensures the continuity and sustainability of the program.

Training

Horse training is another key factor. Horses used in equine therapy should have received solid basic training that allows them to respond predictably and safely to cues from therapists and participants. This includes familiarity with voice and touch cues, as well as the specific equipment used in the sessions, such as adapted saddles or safety elements.

A well-trained horse must be accustomed to working in therapeutic environments, which implies handling people who may present atypical movements or behaviors. This level of preparation ensures that the horse can actively collaborate in the therapeutic process, providing an enriching experience for both the participants and the professionals supervising the sessions.

The role of horses in the therapeutic process

Selecting the right horse not only ensures the success of the sessions, but also protects the equine's well-being by preventing them from being subjected to situations for which they are not prepared or that may generate stress. This careful choice lays the foundation for an effective therapeutic relationship, where the horse acts as a trusted companion and an agent of change on the journey to wellness.

In conclusion, the right horse is one that combines a balanced temperament, optimal health and specialized training. These factors, when integrated, ensure a safe, transformative and respectful experience for all involved.

FACILITIES AND EQUIPMENT REQUIRED

The success of an equine-assisted therapy program depends not only on the horses and therapeutic equipment, but also on the facilities and equipment available. A well-designed, accessible and safe environment ensures the well-being of the participants and the equines, while maximizing the effectiveness of the sessions. Every detail counts to create a space that fosters trust, comfort and safety in every interaction.

Accessibility

Accessibility is a priority in equine-assisted therapy facilities. Spaces must be adapted for people with diverse physical needs, ensuring that they can move around comfortably and safely. This includes the installation of **ramps, handrails and accessible restrooms**, as well as wide aisles that allow the use of wheelchairs or mobility equipment.

In addition, the design must ensure that participants can interact with the horses without barriers, from areas where they can ride them with assistance to spaces where they can perform complementary activities such as brushing or feeding.

Areas of Work

The place where the sessions take place should be specially conditioned to minimize risks and provide comfort for both participants and horses. **Soft surfaces**, such as sand or similar materials, are essential to reduce impact in case of falls and provide safe traction for the equines. These areas should be clearly marked and free of obstacles to avoid accidents.

It is advisable to have covered or semi-covered spaces, which allows the continuity of the sessions in adverse weather conditions. In addition, good lighting and ventilation contribute to creating a pleasant and functional environment.

Safety Equipment

Safety is a crucial aspect, and having the right equipment is a must. Each participant should have **helmets and protective vests** of the correct size, designed specifically for equestrian activities. This equipment not only protects us physically, but also provides additional confidence to the participant, especially in the first few sessions.

Therapeutic equipment should include adapted elements, such as special saddles for riders with reduced mobility and reins or saddles designed to facilitate control and stability during sessions. It is also essential to perform regular reviews of this equipment to ensure its optimal condition.

Rest Spaces

Both participants and horses need **quiet areas to rest** between sessions. For participants, these spaces should be comfortable, protected from the elements and equipped with adequate seating, water and shade. These areas allow them to relax, reflect on the session and prepare for subsequent activities.

Horses also need specific areas to rest. These should include clean stables, shade, fresh water and access to areas where they can move freely. Rest is essential to avoid physical and mental exhaustion of the equine, preserving their well-being and readiness for future sessions.

An environment designed for success

When facilities and equipment are properly planned and maintained, an environment is created that is not only safe and functional, but also welcoming and stimulating. This allows both participants and horses to feel comfortable and safe, which in turn facilitates the development of deep and beneficial therapeutic relationships.

In short, the right facilities and equipment are not just add-ons, but essential components of an equine-assisted therapy program that is effective, sustainable and respectful of all involved.

TRAINING OF THE THERAPEUTIC TEAM

The success of equine-assisted therapy depends mostly on the quality and preparation of the therapeutic team. The team must be composed of multidisciplinary professionals whose training and experience ensure a safe, effective and enriching therapeutic practice. Collaboration between experts from different areas is key to addressing the individual needs of the participants and ensure the welfare of the equines.

Professional Competencies

A well-trained therapeutic team should include a combination of specialized skills and knowledge. **Occupational therapists, physical therapists** and **psychologists** play essential roles in designing and supervising programs that address the physical, cognitive and emotional needs of participants. Their expertise allows them to identify specific therapeutic goals and adjust activities according to the individual's progress.

Alongside them, **equine care specialists** are essential to ensure that horses are in optimal physical and emotional condition. These professionals, with specific training in equine therapy, ensure that horses are prepared to participate in therapeutic sessions, monitor their ongoing well-being and help create a safe environment for all involved.

The integration of these professional competencies not only enriches the program, but also ensures that all aspects necessary for the well-being of participants and horses are addressed.

Continuing Education

In a field as dynamic as equine-assisted therapy, **continuing education** is indispensable. Advances in research, new therapeutic techniques and best practices in equine management must be consistently adopted by the team. This includes attending seminars, workshops and conferences, as well as participating in certification and specialization programs.

Regular updating not only ensures that the team keeps up to date with the latest developments, but also encourages evidence-based therapeutic practice, thereby improving outcomes for participants and equine welfare.

Teamwork

Effective collaboration between members of the therapeutic team is another fundamental pillar. Equine-assisted therapy requires clear and open communication between all professionals, ensuring that knowledge is shared and efforts are coordinated to achieve therapeutic goals.

In addition, a cohesive team can adapt quickly to the changing needs of participants or to unforeseen situations, ensuring program continuity and quality. The ability to work together, respecting the contributions of each discipline, creates an enriching professional environment that benefits everyone involved.

A comprehensive and collaborative approach

Training and cohesion of the therapeutic team are essential for an equine therapy program to reach its full potential. By combining specialized skills, a continuous learning attitude and a strong ability to work as a team, practitioners can provide a therapeutic experience that is transformative for both participants and horses.

Ultimately, a well-prepared team not only ensures the safety and effectiveness of the sessions, but also reinforces the confidence of participants, families and the community in the positive impact of this practice.

CONCLUSION

Proper preparation for equine-assisted therapy is a process that demands careful planning and a holistic approach. From the **meticulous selection of the horses**, which ensures their suitability and well-being, to the **adequacy of the facilities**, designed for safety and accessibility, each aspect plays an essential role in the success of the program. In addition, the **multidisciplinary training of the therapeutic team** ensures that the therapeutic objectives are addressed professionally and effectively.

This methodical approach creates an environment in which therapy can take place in a safe, welcoming and transformative way for both participants and equines. The combination of appropriate facilities, a well-trained professional team and trained horses not only protects the well-being of all involved, but also maximizes the therapeutic benefits, setting a standard of quality and commitment to the practice.

Ultimately, preparation for equine-assisted therapy is the foundation upon which life-changing experiences are built, promoting personal growth and physical and emotional well-being in an environment of respect and collaboration. This chapter reaffirms the importance of approaching every detail with responsibility and dedication, laying the groundwork for a sustainable and enriching practice.

WORK METHODOLOGIES

The methodologies of equine-assisted therapy are dynamic and adaptive, designed to address the unique needs of each participant. Although therapeutic goals vary widely, from improvements in physical mobility to emotional strengthening, the process is based on fundamental steps and structured strategies that guide the intervention toward meaningful and sustainable outcomes. These methodologies combine principles from various disciplines, adapting to everyone's progress and response.

A flexible and customized approach

The starting point in any program is a thorough understanding of the specific goals of each participant. This allows the design of a customized approach that combines proven techniques with the flexibility to respond to changing needs. Despite this customization, the methodologies share certain common elements that establish a solid foundation for intervention.

PARTICIPANT EVALUATION

The initial assessment of each participant is an essential pillar in the equine-assisted therapy process. This thorough analysis provides a solid foundation for designing an effective therapeutic program tailored to the individual's specific needs. The **multidisciplinary assessment** ensures that all key areas, from physical health to emotional well-being, are carefully considered before sessions begin.

This assessment involves a variety of professionals, including **occupational therapists, psychologists**, and sometimes **medical specialists**. The goal is to gain a comprehensive understanding of the participant's situation, including aspects such as **medical history, motor skills, communication** abilities and **social interactions**. This detailed approach makes it possible to identify not only specific challenges, but also strengths that can be enhanced during therapy.

In addition to assessing physical and cognitive aspects, the analysis also encompasses the participant's personal goals, which helps align expectations with therapeutic objectives. This process fosters a person-centered approach, ensuring that therapy is not only effective, but also meaningful and relevant to the individual.

DESIGNING A THERAPEUTIC PLAN

With the information gathered during the initial assessment, a personalized therapeutic plan is developed that acts as a road map for the equine therapy sessions. This plan defines **specific goals, strategies** to achieve them and **evaluation methods** to measure progress. Personalization of this plan is critical, as each participant has unique needs and particular goals.

Therapeutic goals can vary widely, from physical aspects such as improving **coordination, balance** and **muscle tone**, to emotional and social achievements such as fostering **communication**, developing

social skills, or reducing **anxiety** and **stress.** These goals are designed to be achievable and measurable, allowing for continuous monitoring of progress.

The therapeutic plan is not static; it is regularly reviewed and adjusted to reflect the participant's progress and to accommodate any changes in needs or goals. This dynamic approach ensures that therapy remains effective and aligned with the individual's expectations and capabilities. In addition, feedback from the participant and his or her family environment can be integrated into the plan, further enriching the therapeutic experience.

BASIC TECHNIQUES AND EXERCISES

Equine therapy integrates a diverse set of techniques and exercises carefully designed to meet the objectives established in the therapeutic plan. These activities not only address physical, emotional and cognitive aspects, but also foster a deep bond between the participant and the horse. Some of the fundamental techniques used in this therapeutic modality are explored below:

Therapeutic Riding

Therapeutic riding is a central technique in equine-assisted therapy, in which the participant rides the equine and works on key areas such as **balance, posture, coordination** and **muscle strength.** During these sessions, the rhythmic movement of the horse stimulates the rider's neuromuscular system, mimicking the natural human gait pattern and facilitating physical rehabilitation.

This technique can be adapted to the specific needs of the participant. For example, riding styles, such as English or Western, and the use of specialized equipment, such as adapted saddles or modified reins, are selected to address particular challenges. In addition, exercises may include position changes, turns and stretches that strengthen the musculature and improve flexibility.

Horse Care

Activities related to **horse care** are essential to promote the development of motor skills, empathy and responsibility. These tasks include **brushing**, **feeding** and **cleaning the horse**, which not only engages the participant physically, but also strengthens their emotional connection with the animal.

These activities help develop **fine motor skills** through precise and repetitive movements, such as holding a brush or handling cleaning tools. They also foster **patience**, **confidence** and the ability to assume responsibility, since caring for a living being requires constant attention and commitment.

Floor Exercises

Exercises on the ground are a valuable alternative for those participants who, for physical, emotional or confidence reasons, are unable to ride initially. These activities include guiding the horse through a structured trail, where the participant learns to establish effective non-verbal communication and builds mutual trust with the equine. Breathing and relaxation exercises are also performed in the presence of the horse, using its natural calm to induce a state of tranquility and reduce stress. In addition, playful and creative activities involving the animal are carried out, such as interactive games that strengthen teamwork and creativity.

These techniques from the ground are not only effective in developing social and emotional skills, but also provide the participant with a meaningful and accessible therapeutic experience, while establishing a deeper bond with the horse.

A holistic and adaptable approach

Each of these techniques and exercises is carefully selected based on the individual goals of the participant, ensuring a meaningful and personalized therapeutic experience. Their implementation not only addresses physical needs, but also emotional and social aspects, consolidating equine-assisted therapy as an integral and transformative modality.

Ultimately, these activities, whether on the horse or from the ground, constitute a dynamic and flexible framework that facilitates progress in multiple dimensions of the participant's well-being, while strengthening the bond with the horse as a unique therapeutic partner.

MOTOR AND PHYSICAL DEVELOPMENT

Equine therapy is a powerful tool for rehabilitation and physical strengthening, as it uses the natural movement of the equine to effectively stimulate different areas of the body. This unique approach, based on the three-dimensional and rhythmic movement of the horse, allows working on key aspects of motor and physical development, significantly improving the quality of life of the participants.

Balance Exercises

Balance is a fundamental pillar of equine-assisted therapy. During the sessions, the participant performs exercises involving position changes and dynamic tasks on the horse, such as reaching for objects at different heights, leaning forward or sideways, or rotating the torso while maintaining posture. These activities not only strengthen **body stability**, but also develop **proprioception** and **spatial awareness**, essential skills for moving safely in the everyday environment.

The horse's movement acts as a continuous stimulus to the vestibular system, which is responsible for balance and orientation. Each step of the equine challenges the rider to adjust his posture, promoting an adaptive response that enhances the body's ability to maintain control in the face of unpredictable situations. This process contributes to increased confidence in the participant's ability to move, both in the therapeutic context and in daily life.

Muscle Strengthening

The movement of the horse not only stimulates balance, but also activates a wide range of muscle groups simultaneously. Maintaining proper posture while riding requires continuous use of the trunk muscles, such as the abdomen, back and deep stabilizing muscles. This strengthening contributes to **better body posture**, reducing tension and promoting motor control.

In addition, by performing specific exercises, such as holding the reins, changing position or making controlled leg movements, the participant works additional muscles, including those of the upper and lower extremities. For example, the control required to lead the horse activates the muscles of the arms and shoulders, while maintaining contact with the stirrups strengthens the legs and improves body alignment.

The positive impact of muscle strengthening extends to the participant's functional capacity, allowing them to improve in everyday activities, such as walking, getting up or performing more complex movements with greater precision and less effort.

Synergy between Movement and Therapy

Equine-assisted therapy takes advantage of the **synergy between the movement of the horse and the response of the human body**, offering a unique therapeutic experience. This approach not only allows working on specific areas, such as balance or muscle strength, but also integrates these elements in a holistic process of physical and emotional improvement.

The horse becomes a therapeutic ally that constantly stimulates motor development, helping to overcome physical limitations and reinforcing the participant's confidence in his or her own abilities. This adaptive and dynamic approach transforms movement into a healing and empowering tool, highlighting the crucial role of equine therapy in holistic rehabilitation.

SOCIAL AND EMOTIONAL SKILLS

Equine-assisted therapy not only addresses physical and motor aspects, but also has a profound impact on participants' social and emotional skills. Interactions with the horse and activities designed around its care and handling promote the development of a meaningful emotional connection and foster essential life skills.

Horse Care and Management

Actively participating in horse care is more than just a physical activity; it is an opportunity to develop a unique emotional connection and strengthen social skills. Tasks such as **brushing the horse's coat, feeding** and **preparing the horse for sessions** instill a sense of **responsibility** and **commitment**. These activities require patience and attention to detail, fostering the ability to care for and respect another living being.

The emotional bonding that is generated through these tasks is also transformative. The horse, as a non-judgmental being, allows participants to explore their emotions in a safe environment. This type of interaction can be particularly beneficial for people who face difficulties expressing their feelings or who have experienced emotional challenges, such as anxiety, depression or trauma.

In addition, horse handling requires **non-verbal communication skills**, as the animal responds to clear and consistent signals. This interaction helps participants develop a better understanding of how their actions and attitudes affect others, promoting greater **empathy** and **social awareness**.

Reliance Activities

Activities designed to build trust are an essential part of equine-assisted therapy. Exercises such as **leading a horse around a course without riding it** offer a unique experience of collaboration between the participant and the animal. These activities require the participant to establish a **genuine connection** with the horse, using clear and confident cues to direct the horse. This process not only reinforces the participant's confidence in his or her own abilities, but also fosters mutual trust between human and equine.

These experiences help improve **non-verbal communication**, as the horse responds primarily to the participant's body language and energy signals. This type of interaction teaches the importance of **clarity** and **consistency** in communication, skills that are transferable to other social contexts.

When working with the horse, participants also face challenges that can strengthen their **self-esteem**. Overcoming initial nervousness, learning to guide the animal and experiencing success in these activities provides a powerful sense of accomplishment, which can extend to other areas of life.

A Safe Environment for Personal Growth

The horse acts as an emotional mediator that facilitates the development of social and emotional skills in a safe and supportive environment. The therapy not only strengthens the ability to form meaningful bonds, but also empowers participants to face challenges with confidence and resilience. This holistic approach highlights the unique ability of equine-assisted therapy to transform lives, not only physically, but also emotionally.

Cognitive and communication skills

Equine-assisted therapy not only benefits physical and emotional development, but also has a significant impact on cognitive and communication skills. Through carefully designed activities, participants can improve their attention span, memory, decision-making and language skills, all while building a connection with the horse.

Games and Structured Activities

Games and activities during therapeutic sessions are designed to stimulate **problem solving, following instructions** and **decision making**. For example, participants may go through mazes with the horse, identify and name objects located in the environment, or perform tasks in a specific sequence. These activities not only promote cognitive development, but also enhance language skills by involving verbal and nonverbal communication.

The act of planning and executing a task in collaboration with the horse allows participants to exercise their **logical thinking** and **organizational** skills, while strengthening their ability to adapt to new challenges and contexts.

Attention and Concentration Exercises

Horseback riding demands a high level of **attention and concentration**. From maintaining balance to directing the animal with precise signals, each action requires sustained focus. To reinforce these skills, tasks that involve memorizing routes or executing sequences of actions while mounted are integrated. These activities not only improve **sustained attention**, but also foster a greater **mind-body connection**, helping the participants stay present and focused.

The dynamic therapy environment, with constant stimuli from the horse's movement and the surrounding environment, also challenges participants to filter out distractions and focus on the tasks at hand, strengthening their ability to manage multiple stimuli.

<u>**Adaptation of Exercises to Specific Needs**</u>

One of the most outstanding features of equine-assisted therapy is its flexibility to **adapt to the individual needs of each participant.** Exercises and activities are designed to address specific goals, adjusting to the individual's physical, cognitive and communicative abilities.

For example, for a participant seeking to improve communication skills, activities might focus on horse care and tasks that require **following verbal instructions**, encouraging language development and the ability to express oneself. On the other hand, for someone facing physical challenges, such as muscle weakness, exercises might focus on strengthening specific muscle groups through tasks involving balance and posture.

A Personalized and Transformative Approach

The ability to tailor sessions to the specific needs of each participant illustrates the depth and versatility of equine therapy. From cognitive development to improved communication, this therapeutic modality proves to be a comprehensive tool that addresses a wide range of goals, helping participants overcome obstacles and reach their full potential.

This individualized approach not only maximizes therapeutic benefits, but also ensures that each session is meaningful and relevant, reaffirming the transformative impact of the human-horse connection.

SAFETY IN EQUINOTHERAPY

Safety is the fundamental pillar of any therapeutic program based on interaction with horses. Beyond protecting both participants and equines, it is the basis for ensuring effective and enriching sessions. A safe environment allows all involved to fully focus on the goals of the therapy, leaving aside concerns about potential risks. The interactive and dynamic nature of this therapeutic practice demands a careful, rigorous and multidimensional approach to address safety in all its dimensions.

The concept of safety in this context goes beyond the simple physical handling of the animals. It includes essential aspects such as **specialized training of the therapeutic team, proper selection of horses** and **optimal maintenance of the facilities**. In addition, it requires the implementation of **clear and specific protocols** to minimize any risk, taking care of both the welfare of the participants and the horses.

Safety also has an emotional component, which is essential to the success of these sessions. Creating an environment of trust and tranquility is crucial so that participants can fully interact with the horses, explore their emotions and achieve their therapeutic goals in a stress-free space.

KNOWLEDGE AND HANDLING OF HORSES

Proper horse management is an essential component to ensure the safety and effectiveness of any equine-assisted therapeutic program. The human-equine relationship is based on mutual understanding and effective communication, aspects that depend directly on the knowledge and skills of the therapeutic team.

Understanding Equine Behavior

Horses are sensitive animals, whose reactions are deeply linked to their environment and the emotions of those around them. Therefore, understanding their **natural behavior** is crucial. Staff must be able to interpret the signals that horses communicate through their **body language**, such as the movement of their ears, the position of their tails or changes in their posture. These signals, although subtle, can reveal emotional states such as stress, discomfort or calmness.

This knowledge makes it possible to anticipate possible risk situations and to manage interactions in a safe and respectful manner. It also fosters a deeper and more harmonious relationship between horses and participants, creating an environment of mutual trust.

Safe Driving Training

Specific training in safe handling techniques is essential for all personnel involved. This includes learning how to approach the horse properly and without invading the horse's space, which reduces the risk of unexpected reactions. Fitting and removing equipment, such as saddles and straps, must be done with precision and care, ensuring that the horse is always comfortable.

During the sessions, knowing how to lead the horse firmly but gently is fundamental to maintain effective control without generating tension in the animal. These techniques not only protect the participants and the team, but also ensure that the horses remain in an optimal physical and emotional state, indispensable for their role in therapy.

DESIGN AND MAINTENANCE OF FACILITIES

The quality and safety of the facilities are fundamental pillars to ensure a safe and efficient therapeutic environment. A properly designed space not only minimizes risks, but also contributes to the success of the sessions by providing an environment that promotes confidence and comfort for all involved.

Adequate facilities

The design of work areas should focus on maximizing safety for both participants and horses. Therapy areas should have **sturdy, well-installed fences** that delineate interaction spaces, preventing the possibility of horses escaping or encountering outside distractions. **Floors of sand or similar materials**, designed to cushion potential falls, are a must in areas where mounted activities or ground exercises are performed.

It is also essential to keep the area free of sharp objects, hazardous materials or anything that could pose a risk. Storage areas should be organized and out of reach of the horses, while aisles and entrances should be wide and clear enough to allow for safe movement of both equines and participants.

<u>**Regular Maintenance**</u>

Periodic maintenance is an essential task to prevent accidents and ensure the functionality of the facilities. This includes **routine inspection** of fences, gates and any structure that delimits or controls the workspace. Repairing any damage or wear and tear in a timely manner avoids major problems that could endanger those involved.

Riding equipment, such as saddles, reins and straps, should also be checked regularly for wear, breakage or defects that may compromise their safety. In addition, any material or tools used in the sessions should be kept in optimal conditions, making sure they are clean, functional and properly stored.

A consistent focus on facility design and maintenance not only creates a safe environment, but also reinforces confidence in the program, underscoring the therapeutic team's commitment to excellence and care for all participants and animals involved.

SECURITY PROTOCOLS

The implementation of clear and effective safety protocols is essential to ensure a safe and controlled therapeutic environment. These protocols not only prevent risks, but also prepare participants and staff to act efficiently in unforeseen situations, reinforcing confidence in the program.

Protocol Development

Having **well-defined and communicated safety rules** is crucial to the success of any equine-assisted program. These protocols should range from procedures for **safe entry and exit of work areas** to rules for **behavior around horses**. For example, participants should know how to approach horses without invading their personal space and understand what actions could cause stress or unexpected reactions.

In addition, it is essential to establish clear procedures for **emergency response**, including specific instructions for action in case of accidents, injuries or situations that may endanger horses or participants. Accessibility to the protocols, through posters or explanatory documents, ensures that everyone, from the therapeutic team to visitors, understands the essential rules.

Emergency Drills

Practical preparation is essential so that the protocols not only exist in theory, but can be effectively applied. Conducting **regular drills** allows the therapeutic team and participants to become familiar with the procedures necessary in emergency situations. This includes practicing **quick and orderly evacuations**, learning how to administer **basic first aid**, and fostering **clear and efficient communication** during times of stress.

These exercises not only improve the response capacity of the personnel, but also generate confidence in the participants, who feel safer knowing that the program is prepared to protect them. In addition, periodically evaluating the drills helps to identify areas for improvement and to keep the protocols up to date in the face of possible changes in the facilities or program dynamics.

Together, the safety protocols and regular drills form a solid foundation to ensure that each therapy session is conducted in a controlled, safe environment that is prepared for any eventuality.

PERSONAL PROTECTIVE EQUIPMENT

The use of personal protective equipment is an essential element to ensure safety in equine-assisted therapy sessions. This equipment not only protects participants from possible accidents, but also promotes an environment where safety is a priority in all activities.

Mandatory Use of Protective Equipment

The **use of approved safety helmets** should be a mandatory requirement for all participants, regardless of their level of experience or the activities they perform. These helmets are specifically designed to cushion impacts and protect the head in case of falls, one of the most common risk situations in interactions with horses.

In addition to helmets, **suitable boots with reinforced toe caps and non-slip soles** are a must. This type of footwear protects the feet from accidental stomping and ensures a good grip on uneven or slippery surfaces. Also, depending on the specific needs of the session, protective vests may be considered, especially for people participating in mounted activities.

<u>**Equipment Selection and Maintenance**</u>

Proper selection of equipment is crucial. All equipment must meet established safety standards and be properly fitted to the participant's measurements to ensure its effectiveness. A helmet that is too large or boots that do not fit properly may compromise safety more than protect it.

Regular maintenance of equipment is equally important. Helmets should be inspected periodically for cracks or other damage, and any equipment showing signs of significant wear should be replaced immediately. Boots and other accessories also require constant cleaning and checking to ensure they are in top condition.

Promoting a culture of safety around the use of equipment not only physically protects participants, but also reinforces the importance of taking precautions in all activities, laying the foundation for a safe and reliable therapeutic experience.

FIRST AID TRAINING

First aid training is an essential skill for all personnel involved in therapeutic programs involving horses. This training not only ensures a quick and effective response to possible accidents, but also contributes to creating an environment of trust and safety for both participants and animals.

General First Aid Training

The entire therapeutic team must have basic knowledge of first aid, such as how to handle cuts, bruises, sprains or medical emergencies, such as fainting or anxiety attacks. This type of training allows immediate action to be taken while awaiting the arrival of professional medical services, thus ensuring that any incident is attended to in a timely and effective manner.

First Aid Related to Horses

In the specific context of equine-assisted therapy, it is essential to include training in **first aid specific to equine injuries**. This could include initial treatment of superficial wounds, immobilization of limbs in case of fractures, and safe handling in situations where the horse is stressed or startled. Staff should also be prepared to deal with human injuries related to horse handling, such as bites, trampling or falls.

Regular Drills and Updates

Training should not be limited to a single instance; **regular updates** are crucial to ensure that the team is up to date with best practices and protocols. Regular drills are also useful to prepare personnel for real-life situations, allowing them to practice critical skills in a controlled environment.

This preparation not only minimizes risks, but also sends a clear message of professionalism and commitment to the well-being of all involved, from the participants to the horses, reinforcing confidence in the program and peace of mind for families who rely on this type of therapeutic intervention.

CASE STUDIES AND APPLICATIONS

Equine-assisted therapy has proven to be a powerful tool in a variety of contexts, addressing physical, emotional, cognitive and social challenges. Its ability to adapt to the specific needs of each individual makes it a highly versatile modality. In this chapter, we will explore two case studies that highlight the benefits and applicability of this therapeutic intervention.

Versatility and Effectiveness in Different Contexts

The impact of equine therapy is manifested in its ability to customize interventions according to the unique characteristics of each participant. This flexibility makes it possible to treat everything from physical conditions such as cerebral palsy, to emotional disorders such as depression, to cognitive and social developmental needs in people with autism spectrum disorders.

In this chapter, we will take an in-depth look at two case studies that reflect how this practice transforms lives, showing the therapeutic reach that can be achieved by combining technical knowledge with the unique connection that is established between humans and horses.

CASE STUDY 1:

EQUINE THERAPY IN AUTISM SPECTRUM DISORDERS

Carlos, an 8-year-old boy with a diagnosis of autism spectrum disorder (ASD), began receiving equine-assisted therapy as an adjunct to his conventional therapeutic interventions. This decision was based on the need to address specific challenges related to communication, social interaction and emotional self-regulation.

Therapeutic Intervention

From the first sessions, the focus was on carefully designed activities that promoted eye contact, non-verbal communication and building a bond of trust with the horse. Carlos participated in exercises such as leading the horse on the ground and performing basic grooming tasks, such as brushing. These activities provided him with predictable structure, which is crucial for children with ASD, while the horse acted as a positive and constant stimulus.

Observed Results

Over time, Carlos showed significant progress. His therapists noted an improvement in his ability to follow simple instructions, as well as an increase in his willingness to maintain eye contact with the therapist and the horse. These improvements in nonverbal communication represented an important step toward greater social interaction.

At home, his mother reported noticeable changes in Carlos' behavior, including a decrease in episodes of self-isolation and an increase in his confidence to explore new activities. The bond that Carlos developed with the horse also appeared to play a key role in these gains, as it allowed him to experience a sense of accomplishment and connection in a safe, non-judgmental environment.

Lessons from the Case

This case highlights how equine therapy can serve as a valuable complement to traditional therapies for individuals with ASD. By providing a structured, human-animal bond-centered environment, it facilitates the development of essential skills and promotes tangible emotional progress. In addition, this holistic approach reinforces the importance of tailoring activities to the individual needs of each participant, maximizing therapeutic impact.

CASE STUDY 2:

TRAUMA HEALING THROUGH EQUINE-ASSISTED THERAPY

Ana, a 35-year-old veteran experiencing post-traumatic stress disorder (PTSD) following her military service, found interaction with horses a unique and effective avenue to address the traumas that had profoundly impacted her daily life. Equine-assisted therapy provided her with a safe, non-judgmental environment to explore difficult emotions and rebuild her sense of confidence.

Therapeutic Intervention

From the beginning, Ana was paired with a horse known for his calm and responsive temperament. The therapeutic approach focused on grooming tasks, such as brushing and leading him on the ground, before introducing therapeutic riding. These activities allowed Ana to connect with the horse on an emotional level, creating a space where she could process feelings of vulnerability and work on building mutual trust.

The therapist guided the sessions with reflective questions and mindfulness techniques, helping Ana to remain present in the moment while interacting with the horse. This direct connection with the animal allowed her to face her fears in a controlled and manageable way, offering a tangible way to experience calmness and self-efficacy.

Observed Results

Throughout the sessions, Ana showed a marked reduction in the intensity of PTSD-related symptoms, including hypervigilance and anxiety episodes. The interaction with the horse became a catalyst for improving her ability to manage stress and reestablish an emotional connection with others, something that had proven difficult due to her traumatic experience.

One of the most significant breakthroughs occurred when Ana felt comfortable enough to participate in more complex riding exercises. This marked a turning point in her recovery process, as she began to identify progress because of her effort and the trusting relationship built with the horse.

<u>**Lessons from the Case**</u>

Ana's case highlights how equine-assisted therapy can be a transformative tool in recovery from emotional trauma. The interaction with the horse provided a practical and experiential approach to processing complex emotions, offering a valuable complement to other forms of psychological therapy.

It also stresses the importance of carefully selecting horses and activities to suit the individual needs of the participant, thus maximizing the emotional and psychological benefits of this intervention.

HORSE WELFARE MAINTENANCE

The welfare of horses in therapeutic programs is much more than just an ethical obligation; it is an essential requirement to ensure the effectiveness and safety of equine-assisted therapy. A horse that is physically and emotionally healthy can not only perform its role optimally, but also contributes to a positive and enriching environment for the participants.

The Importance of Equine Welfare

Comprehensive horse care encompasses several interrelated areas, including the horse's physical health, feeding, exercise, housing and emotional needs. Each of these aspects is crucial to ensure that the horse is in optimal condition to interact with the participants and respond appropriately during the sessions.

This chapter delves into the key components that ensure the welfare of the horse, highlighting how each element impacts both the animal and the overall quality of the therapeutic program. In addition, practices and recommendations for maintaining high standards of equine care, promoting longevity and emotional balance of the animal in this therapeutic context will be explored.

LODGING AND ENVIRONMENT

The housing and the environment in which horses live are essential components to ensure their optimal well-being and performance in a therapeutic program. A well-designed and maintained environment not only ensures the physical health of the horses, but also promotes their emotional and social balance.

Stables and Shelters

Stables should meet standards that ensure the comfort and safety of the horse. Each space should be **spacious and well ventilated**, allowing the horse to lie down, turn around and move easily. Natural light is essential to maintain the balance of the horse's circadian rhythm, while good ventilation reduces the risk of respiratory disease.

In addition, barns should be kept clean by regular routine manure removal and bedding renewal. This not only improves animal comfort, but also prevents infections and other health problems. To complement the stables, it is important to have **outdoor shelters** that offer protection from the sun, rain or wind. These spaces allow horses to rest outdoors in a safe and natural environment.

Grazing and Exercise Areas

Access to **extensive grazing areas** is crucial for horses, as it promotes their physical and emotional well-being. Grazing provides them with a natural activity, while regular exercise, such as running or walking, helps maintain their physical condition and prevents muscle or joint problems.

These areas also play an important role in the emotional well-being of the horse. Horses are social animals that thrive in the company of other equines. Providing them with a space where they can interact with their peers encourages natural behavior, reduces stress and contributes to maintaining a balanced emotional state.

Conclusion

The combination of adequate stables, outdoor shelters and well-designed grazing areas creates a holistic environment that caters to the horses' physical, social and emotional needs. This approach ensures that they can perform effectively and safely in therapeutic sessions, while enjoying an optimal quality of life.

FOOD AND NUTRITION

Proper nutrition is an essential pillar in the care of horses in therapeutic programs. A balanced diet and a well-structured feeding program not only ensure the physical health of the animal, but also directly influence its emotional well-being and performance in therapeutic sessions.

Balanced Diet

The basis of proper nutrition for horses is **high quality forage**, such as hay or fresh grass, which makes up the majority of their diet. This component is essential for maintaining a healthy digestive system and preventing problems such as colic or gastric ulcers. In addition to forage, grains can be included in controlled amounts to supplement the horse's energy needs, especially for horses that perform more demanding activities.

Each horse has unique requirements depending on its age, weight, activity level and health status. In some cases, it may be necessary to include **nutritional supplements**, such as vitamins, minerals or specific oils, to ensure that the animal receives all the necessary nutrients. These supplements should be administered under the supervision of a veterinarian or equine nutritionist.

Constant access to **fresh, clean water** is essential. A horse can consume between 20 and 40 liters of water per day, and adequate hydration is essential for the optimal functioning of all body systems.

Regular Food Program

Horses are animals that thrive on routine. Feeding them at the **same times each day** helps stabilize their metabolism, reduce stress and prevent digestive problems. Dividing meals into several small portions throughout the day mimics their natural eating patterns and improves digestion.

In addition, the environment in which the horse is fed should be quiet and safe to minimize distractions or conflicts with other horses, which ensures that each animal receives the proper amount of food without unnecessary stress.

Conclusion

Balanced nutrition and a consistent feeding program are fundamental to maintaining the health and well-being of horses. This approach not only enables them to perform their therapeutic role effectively, but also contributes to their overall quality of life, ensuring that they can optimally respond to the physical and emotional demands of equine-assisted therapy.

HEALTH CARE

Maintaining the physical health of horses is a crucial component in their overall well-being, especially in the context of assisted therapy. Therapeutic programs depend on healthy horses in optimal condition to ensure safe and effective sessions. The following are key aspects of equine health care.

Regular Veterinary Checkups

Regular veterinary checkups are essential to prevent disease and treat any condition before it becomes a major problem. A well-planned veterinary care program includes **routine vaccinations** to protect horses against common diseases and **periodic deworming** to prevent internal and external infections.

In addition, **dental care** plays an essential role in the overall health of the horse. Regular examination and maintenance of the teeth by a specialist ensures efficient chewing, which is vital for proper digestion and nutritional well-being.

Hull Care

Hooves are essential for the horse's mobility and well-being. **Regular maintenance by a professional farrier** is essential to prevent problems such as cracks, infections or deformities that can affect the animal's locomotion. This includes periodic hoof trimming and shoeing when necessary, depending on the horse's environment and activities.

Constant monitoring of hoof condition allows early identification and treatment of problems, ensuring that the horse can perform its therapeutic activities without pain or discomfort.

Conclusion

Comprehensive equine health care, encompassing both veterinary care and hoof maintenance, is critical to the success of any equine therapeutic program. These efforts not only ensure the animal's physical well-being, but also create a solid foundation for its performance as a reliable and effective therapeutic companion.

EMOTIONAL WELL-BEING

The emotional well-being of horses is as essential as their physical health to ensure their ability to participate in therapeutic programs effectively and safely. Horses, as social and intelligent beings, thrive in environments that meet their emotional needs, fostering their mental balance and willingness to interact with participants.

Interaction and Mental Stimulation

Horses need activities that stimulate their minds and keep them interested, avoiding boredom and stress. **Mental stimulation** can be achieved using toys designed specifically for horses, which challenge their natural curiosity and provide them with opportunities to explore.

In addition, **varied training**, including different exercises and activities, keeps their routines dynamic and builds their confidence.

Quality time with humans and other horses is also vital. Social interactions between horses contribute to natural and balanced behavior, while positive relationships with humans reinforce trust and willingness to participate in therapeutic sessions. These emotional connections strengthen the horse-human bond, improving the quality of the sessions.

Respectful and Consistent Management

Daily management should be based on a respectful and consistent approach. Treating the horse with gentleness and patience not only reinforces the horse's trust in humans, but also reduces the risk of defensive or aggressive responses. **Consistency in daily routines** is key to providing a predictable and safe environment, minimizing stress.

Horses thrive in environments where they understand what to expect from their caretakers. This includes clear interactions, regular feeding and resting times, and management that prioritizes their well-being over convenience. Consistency and respect not only contribute to a horse's emotional balance, but also prepare them to participate in therapeutic activities with greater confidence and willingness.

<u>Conclusion</u>

The emotional well-being of horses is fundamental to their role in assisted therapy. Providing them with a stimulating environment, respectful handling and opportunities to develop deep bonds ensures that they are mentally and emotionally fit to participate in therapeutic sessions. This holistic approach not only benefits the horses, but also

reflects an ethical commitment to their care, modeling a relationship of respect and harmony between humans and animals.

PROFESSIONAL DEVELOPMENT IN EQUINE THERAPY

Entering the field of equine-assisted therapy (OT) requires more than a passion for animals and an interest in human welfare. The field demands a deep commitment to continuing education, the acquisition of technical skills, and an understanding of the ethical and practical principles that guide this practice. Being an equine therapy practitioner involves not only working with horses, but also interacting with people who present a wide range of physical, emotional and cognitive needs.

TRAINING AND CERTIFICATION ROUTES

Academic Background

The path to a career in equine-assisted therapy begins with a solid academic background. Disciplines such as occupational therapy, physical therapy, psychology and veterinary medicine provide an essential foundation for understanding and addressing the needs of participants. Educational programs in these areas integrate knowledge of human development, physical rehabilitation, mental health and animal behavior. In addition, many universities and specialized centers offer specific courses in animal-assisted therapy, combining theory with practice designed to apply therapeutic strategies in an equine context.

<u>**Specialized Certifications**</u>

Certification is an essential step in ensuring quality and ethics in professional practice. Organizations such as PATH International focus on areas such as therapeutic riding and equine management, offering comprehensive programs that combine theoretical and practical training. Eagala, specializing in mental health and personal development, trains professionals to integrate human-horse interaction in therapeutic and educational contexts. HETI promotes international standards, fosters a global network of therapists and ensures that professionals participate in continuing education to keep up with the latest research and advances in the field.

KEY COMPETENCIES FOR PROFESSIONALS

<u>**Interpersonal Skills**</u>

Empathy and effective communication are fundamental for any equine-assisted therapy practitioner. The ability to build trusting relationships with participants, their families and the interdisciplinary team not only strengthens the therapeutic process, but also creates a safe and nurturing environment. These skills allow therapists to connect deeply with the emotions and needs of participants, fostering a supportive environment where therapeutic goals can be achieved more effectively.

<u>**Expertise in Horses**</u>

A thorough knowledge of horse behavior, care and handling is essential to ensure the safety and effectiveness of therapeutic sessions. Understanding horses' body language, temperament, and physical and emotional needs allows practitioners to anticipate and manage situations proactively. This specialized knowledge not only promotes respectful and harmonious interaction, but also ensures that horses are in optimal condition to participate in therapeutic interventions.

Development of an Integrated Therapeutic Approach

Integrating knowledge from various disciplines, such as psychology, physiotherapy and occupational therapy, is crucial to tailoring therapeutic approaches to the specific needs of each participant. This multidisciplinary approach allows professionals to design personalized intervention plans that address both the physical and emotional aspects of the participants, thus optimizing therapy outcomes.

ESTABLISHING A SUCCESSFUL PRACTICE

Entrepreneurship and Business Management

Starting and managing an equine-assisted therapy practice requires a sound approach to business planning and financial sustainability. Establishing clear objectives, developing a detailed business plan and defining an efficient operational structure are the first steps to success. Incorporating marketing strategies aimed at highlighting the unique benefits of equine-assisted therapy can increase visibility and attract new participants. In addition, quality assurance must be a constant priority, ensuring that sessions are conducted under strict ethical and professional standards. Financial sustainability is achieved by balancing operating costs with affordable fees, diversifying revenue sources and managing resources effectively.

<u>**Networking and Collaboration**</u>

The success of an equine-assisted therapy practice also depends on the ability to build a strong professional network. Establishing collaborations with therapists, clinicians, educators and community organizations allows for broadening the scope of practice and enriching therapeutic interventions. Participating in industry events, attending conferences and joining professional associations are effective strategies for staying current with the latest trends and strengthening connections within the field. These alliances not only promote a steady flow of referrals, but also foster a supportive professional community that shares resources and knowledge.

CONTINUOUS PROFESSIONAL DEVELOPMENT

<u>**Continuing Education**</u>

Lifelong learning is essential to stay on the cutting edge in the field of equine-assisted therapy. Continuing education allows practitioners to incorporate the latest research and therapeutic techniques into their practice, ensuring an evidence-based approach. In addition, participating in advanced courses and specialization programs enhances the quality of therapeutic interventions and reinforces the confidence of participants and their families in the services offered.

<u>**Participation in the Professional Community**</u>

Actively engaging in the professional community is a powerful way to enrich practice and contribute to the development of the field. Attending conferences and workshops provides opportunities to learn from experts, exchange experiences and explore new perspectives. Joining professional organizations not only offers access to exclusive resources, but also fosters collaboration and support among colleagues, strengthening a robust professional network.

Research and Contribution to the Field

Participation in research related to equine-assisted therapy plays a fundamental role in the advancement of this discipline. Professionals who collaborate in scientific studies contribute to the development of new therapeutic methods and the validation of existing ones, establishing a solid knowledge base. In addition, publishing findings and sharing experiences through academic journals and events helps to expand the understanding and acceptance of this therapeutic modality globally.

FUTURE OF EQUINE THERAPY

The horizon of equine-assisted therapy promises dynamic development, driven by the integration of innovative approaches and the evolution of existing practices. This therapeutic modality, which has already proven to be transformative, is constantly growing, expanding its scope and effectiveness in response to the demands of a changing society.

As scientific research advances, the understanding of human-animal interaction deepens, providing a more solid foundation for the design of personalized therapeutic programs. This integration of knowledge will allow us to explore new ways of applying the benefits of the human-horse relationship, both in traditional contexts and in emerging areas of health and wellness.

The future will also be marked by the incorporation of advanced technologies, such as biometric monitoring devices to assess the physiological and emotional impact of sessions. These tools will provide valuable data that will not only validate the benefits of equine-assisted therapy, but also allow for real-time adjustments to optimize interventions.

In addition, the growing acceptance of this practice in educational and mental health settings suggests an expansion in its implementation at the community and institutional level. With the collaboration of professionals from various disciplines, this therapy is positioned to address complex challenges such as post-traumatic stress, neurodevelopmental disorders and emotional conditions with a holistic approach.

The road to the future of equine-assisted therapy is not only filled with opportunities, but also with responsibilities. Its evolution requires a continued commitment to ethics, sustainability and the welfare of the horses that make this transformation possible in the lives of so many people. This exciting development ensures that this therapeutic modality will continue to make a significant difference in human well-being, while inspiring a deeper respect for the unique connection between humans and horses.

INNOVATION AND TECHNOLOGY

The integration of emerging technologies is transforming the way equine-assisted therapeutic interventions are implemented, expanding their reach and improving their effectiveness. Tools such as virtual reality (VR) are opening new possibilities, allowing people with physical limitations or in inaccessible environments to experience the benefits of interaction with horses. These simulations can recreate sensations of riding and related activities, providing similar therapeutic effects in terms of cognitive, emotional and motor stimulation.

Another significant innovation is the use of advanced motion tracking systems and biometric sensors. These devices provide detailed, real-time analysis of the interaction between horse and participant, measuring variables such as posture, balance and emotional response. This data-driven approach allows sessions to be adjusted to maximize their therapeutic impact, in addition to scientifically validating the results obtained.

In addition, digital platforms are facilitating the training and certification of equine therapy practitioners, enabling broader access to knowledge and fostering global collaboration in the development of best practices. These technologies expand opportunities for participants and raise standards of practice by integrating innovative methods into a field deeply rooted in tradition.

The adoption of these tools represents a bold step into the future of equine-assisted therapy, showing how technology can complement and enrich the transformative impact of human-animal interaction.

RESEARCH ADVANCES

Research in equine-assisted therapy is rapidly evolving, focusing on understanding both the therapeutic benefits to participants and the impact these interactions have on horses. This holistic approach is expanding knowledge about how human-equine dynamics can be optimized to maximize therapeutic outcomes.

Recent studies are analyzing the physiological and emotional responses of horses during therapy sessions. This research reveals how factors such as handling, frequency of sessions and environmental conditions affect the well-being of the animals. This knowledge is not only helping to scientifically validate the benefits of equine-assisted therapy, but is also leading to the development of more ethical and sustainable practices.

In addition, neuroscience research is providing insights into how interactions with horses influence participants' brain processes, including emotional regulation, stress reduction and improved attention. This evidence-based approach is strengthening the therapy's credibility in medical and psychological communities, encouraging its inclusion in comprehensive treatment programs.

Expanding research in this field not only reinforces the efficacy of this therapeutic modality, but also promotes a more respectful and conscious relationship between humans and horses, ensuring that both fully benefit from these unique interactions.

APPLICATION EXPANSION

The horizon of equine-assisted therapy is constantly expanding, encompassing new areas of application that respond to a diverse range of therapeutic needs. In the future, this modality may be integrated into addiction recovery programs, offering emotional and physical support to those facing this challenge. In addition, its efficacy in managing disorders such as post-traumatic stress disorder (PTSD) promises to extend to vulnerable populations, including veterans, victims of violence and emergency professionals.

Another area of potential expansion is mental health in young people, where the bond with horses can play a key role in promoting self-esteem, stress management and the development of social skills. Thanks to its adaptability, this therapy will continue to adjust to the specific needs of each participant, consolidating itself as a powerful tool in more diverse and complex therapeutic environments.

EDUCATION AND TRAINING

Equine-assisted therapy training is evolving toward more accessible and rigorous standards. Educational institutions and specialized organizations are developing programs that offer professional certifications and academic degrees, providing future therapists with a solid foundation of knowledge and practical skills.

This improvement in training not only raises the quality of services offered, but also sets higher professional standards within the therapeutic community. As more people specialize in this field, its acceptance in the medical and psychological fields is likely to increase, encouraging broader integration into conventional treatment plans.

Strengthening education in this field also encourages research and the development of new methodologies, ensuring that this practice continues to evolve and remain relevant in an ever-changing therapeutic world. This educational advancement promises to transform equine-assisted therapy into an even more respected and widely recognized field.

COMMUNITY INTEGRATION

The expansion of equine-assisted therapy into community settings such as schools, hospitals and senior centers is redefining its scope and relevance. This approach allows more people, regardless of socioeconomic status or physical limitations, to access the therapeutic benefits of interaction with horses.

In schools, these interventions promote social skills, self-esteem and concentration in students, while in hospitals and senior centers, they offer a unique way to relieve stress, improve mood and support physical rehabilitation. By integrating into diverse community spaces, horses reinforce their role as agents of positive change in the social fabric, transforming lives and fostering a deeper connection between people and the natural world.

CONCLUSION

The future of equine-assisted therapy promises significant growth, supported by technological innovation, advanced research and a renewed commitment to education and ethics. This evolution not only expands its therapeutic potential, but also strengthens its impact on promoting both human and equine wellness.

As this practice continues to adapt to the changing needs of society, its importance as a therapeutic tool will continue to consolidate. The dedication of the professional community in this field ensures that emerging opportunities are seized and challenges are met with creativity and rigor, setting a promising path for future generations.

CONCLUSION

<u>Looking to the future of equine-assisted therapy</u>

As we conclude this journey through the world of equine-assisted therapy, it is clear that this is an ever-expanding discipline that combines tradition and innovation to generate a transformative impact on human and equine well-being. This therapeutic method, which weaves a deep interspecies bond, represents not only a therapeutic alternative, but also a reminder of the power of connection and empathy.

The evolution of this practice, supported by advances in research, adoption of emerging technologies and commitment to the highest ethical standards, opens the door to a future full of possibilities. Each step toward broader integration, more rigorous education and more diversified applications reinforces the value of human-equine interaction as a bridge to healing and growth.

Going forward, equine-assisted therapy will not only continue to make a difference in the lives of those who participate in it, but will also serve as a beacon of hope and collaboration between humans and animals. At its core, this practice embodies the spirit of mutual respect and the pursuit of shared well-being that transcends individual barriers, offering an inspiring vision for the future of integrative therapies.

LEARNING SYNTHESIS

Throughout this guide, we have unraveled the fundamental pillars that underpin equine-assisted therapy, highlighting the key elements that ensure its effectiveness and sustainability. From the careful selection of horses to the creation of safe and adapted environments, every aspect has been designed to maximize therapeutic impact while ensuring the well-being of all involved.

In addition, the relevance of forming multidisciplinary therapeutic teams that integrate knowledge from various disciplines to provide holistic care has been highlighted. This approach reinforces the idea that horses, far from being mere tools, are true therapeutic partners, whose sensitivity and ability to connect deeply with humans represent the core of this practice.

Finally, the emphasis on an ethical approach and mutual respect has been enshrined as a guiding principle. Equine-assisted therapy not only transforms human lives, but also redefines our relationship with these animals, demonstrating that the success of this practice lies in the harmony between care and connection.

PROGRESS AND PERSPECTIVES

The future of equine-assisted intervention looks like fertile ground for innovation and expansion. The incorporation of advanced technologies, such as augmented reality and motion analysis tools, is opening new possibilities for personalizing and diversifying therapies, allowing people with physical or geographic limitations to experience their benefits. This technological approach not only democratizes access, but also offers unprecedented ways to measure and evaluate therapeutic impact in real time.

At the same time, advances in scientific research are illuminating previously unknown aspects of the relationship between humans and horses, deepening the mechanisms that make this therapeutic connection possible. This research not only improves the effectiveness of interventions, but also promotes a more ethical and conscious treatment of horses, integrating them as full participants in the therapeutic process.

THE ROLE OF THE COMMUNITY AND EDUCATION

The consolidation of equine-assisted therapy as a widely accepted and valued practice depends largely on strengthening a committed community of practitioners, researchers and advocates. This community fabric, based on collaboration and knowledge sharing, is key to meeting future challenges and taking advantage of emerging opportunities.

Education is the central axis of this process. Not only through rigorous training of new therapists, but also through awareness programs that highlight the benefits and transformative impact of this therapeutic modality. The integration of these efforts in schools, health centers and communities amplifies their reach, promoting a cultural shift that recognizes and celebrates the unique value of horses as partners in human wellness.

CALL TO ACTION

As we conclude this journey, we extend an invitation to all readers, whether they are health professionals, passionate about horses or simply interested in human welfare, to reflect on how equine-assisted intervention can make a difference in their lives or in the lives of those around them. Participating in this evolution does not necessarily require being a therapist; supporting local programs, promoting this practice in their communities, or even sharing their knowledge and experiences, are significant contributions that can enrich the reach of this therapy.

FINAL REFLECTION

Equine-assisted therapy teaches us about the transformative power of connection, a lesson that transcends human-equine interaction. It invites us to reconnect with our essence, to explore deeper links with the natural world and to rediscover our capacity for empathy and healing. Each session, each step towards a more ethical and inclusive future, is a reminder that true progress lies in the balance between innovation and respect. As we move forward together on this path, we reaffirm our dedication to an approach that values both humans and horses, celebrating the unique bond that makes this therapeutic practice possible.

ACKNOWLEDGMENTS

With gratitude, Aura Hípica thanks the noble horses that inspire our work and the equine-assisted therapy community for their shared wisdom. Special thanks to family, friends and readers for their unwavering support and faith in this project.